ROSIE

A Visiting Dog's Story

ROSIE

A Visiting Dog's Story

by Stephanie Calmenson
photographs by Justin Sutcliffe

Clarion Books

NEW YORK

Clarion Books
a Houghton Mifflin Company imprint
215 Park Avenue South, New York, NY 10003
Text copyright © 1994 by Stephanie Calmenson
Photographs copyright © 1994 by Justin Sutcliffe

The names of Cheerios™, Evian™, and Jell-O™ are officially
registered trademarks, and are legally restricted to the use of
their owners or manufacturers.

Type is 15 pt. Galliard Roman.
Book design by Carol Goldenberg.
Printed in China.

Library of Congress Cataloging-in-Publication Data
Calmenson, Stephanie.
  Rosie, a visiting dog's story / by Stephanie Calmenson ;
photographs by Justin Sutcliffe.
    p.   cm.
ISBN 0-395-65477-7   PA ISBN 0-395-92722-6
1. Dogs—Therapeutic use—Juvenile literature.   [1.Dogs—
Training.   2. Human-animal relationships.]   I. Sutcliffe,
Justin, ill.   II. Title.
RM931.D63C35   1994
636.7—dc20   93-21243
              CIP
              AC

LEO   20 19 18 17 16 15 14 13 12 11
4500209155

~ To Rosie ~

This is Rosie, my dog. She loves to play fetch. She will roll over to have her belly rubbed. And she will lick you on the nose if you are her friend.

Rosie is like many other dogs — maybe even like your
dog. But in one way, Rosie is special.

Rosie is a working dog. Here she is in her uniform. Her red harness and special badges say to everyone, *I am a visiting dog*. A visiting dog's job is to cheer up people who are sad, or sick, or lonely.

Rosie was not always a visiting dog. She had to be trained for her work.

This is how Rosie looked when she was a puppy. You could see her eyes! Rosie the puppy would not have been a good visiting dog. She was too wild and silly.

Rosie liked to snoop. Rosie left puddles in all the wrong places. Rosie chewed everything in sight!

But even as a puppy Rosie was gentle and friendly. And she was a good listener. I knew that Rosie would make a good visiting dog someday.

We started Rosie's training at puppy kindergarten. Robin Kovary was our teacher. She taught me how to teach Rosie.

Robin was firm but always gentle. That was important because Rosie had to trust people. She had to be confident that no one would harm her. Rosie also needed to keep her independent spirit. She might have to make a decision on her own while working one day.

Rosie liked school. She learned her lessons fast.

Rosie, sit. Good dog!

Rosie, down. Good dog!

Rosie, stay. Good dog!

Rosie, come. Good dog!

At home, I tried to prepare Rosie for her work. First, it was important for Rosie to be a happy dog. After all, a sad dog could not cheer anyone up. So we played a lot of games. Her favorites were fetch and "catch-me-if-you-can."

Rosie would also have to get along with other dogs in case she had to work alongside them. So she got plenty of time to play with her friends.

A good visiting dog has to be comfortable with all kinds of people. I introduced Rosie to as many different people as I could.

On one street Rosie would sit quietly with an elderly person.

On the next street she would run and play with a child.

Rosie always had good sense. If a person wanted to play, Rosie played. If a person seemed shy, Rosie would lie down and wait for the person to come to her.

Rosie was ready to join a visiting dog program at the ASPCA when she was two years old. Her real training was about to begin.

Our teacher was Micky Niego. In the class there were big dogs and small dogs, short-haired and long-haired dogs, pedigrees and mixed breeds.

All the dogs had two things in common: They were friendly and they were happy to work.

Micky began the class by having the dogs practice their basic obedience skills: Sit, down, stay, come. Then Micky added new skills.

Rosie learned to "Go say hello." This means that Rosie will not approach a person until she is told that the person is ready to greet her.

She learned the "Don't touch" command. When Rosie hears it she will not touch food or anything else until she hears, "Okay, take it!" It is important for Rosie never to be rude and grab from a person.

The people Rosie would visit might be using wheelchairs and walkers. So Rosie had to be comfortable with all kinds of equipment.

Rosie also had to get used to being handled in different ways. A young child might pull her tail or her long hair, not knowing any better.

An elderly or ill person might pet her too roughly by mistake.

Rosie had to be patient and gentle even at times like these.

Rosie also had to be a good traveler. To get to work, Rosie might need to ride on a train, a bus, or even an airplane. Rosie was given a special travel pass, which allows her to ride with me.

We took many trips together. Rosie learned to be a quiet, well-mannered traveler. And, of course, she made lots of friends.

After four months of training, Rosie and her classmates were tested. Rosie went into a room with volunteers. The volunteers behaved the way the people Rosie would visit might behave.

A little girl with tubes was on a bed. Rosie did not nip at the tubes the way she would have when she was a puppy. Rosie lay quietly by the little girl's side.

A woman dropped a walker in front of Rosie. Rosie did not bark or snap or act fearful. She calmly stepped out of the way.

There were many tests. Rosie passed them all with flying colors!

A few weeks later, Rosie's badges came in the mail. It was time for our first visit. We were invited to a children's hospital.

Before we went, I took Rosie to her vet, Dr. Jimmy Corrao, for a checkup. A visiting dog has to be healthy.

Then I gave Rosie a bath in a special shampoo that made her feel soft and smell sweet.

On the day of our visit, I packed water for Rosie to drink, a soft brush in case someone wanted to groom her, a ball so she could play, and Cheerios to eat. (Cheerios are good for people *and* pets.)

When we went outside, Rosie had on her red harness, her badges, and a big red bow. I could see that Rosie was proud. She held her head up high.

At the children's hospital, David James, the program director, was waiting for us. I introduced myself and then Rosie.

"Rosie, sit. Paw, please," I said.

Rosie gave Mr. James her paw.

"Hello, Rosie," said Mr. James. "I have some friends I want you to meet. Follow me."

Rosie made a lot of new friends that day. Nina is in a wheelchair because she cannot use her legs. But she has a great throwing arm.

"Rosie, fetch!" she called. Nina threw the ball way across the room. Lucky Rosie! She loves to fetch.

Peter, who is blind, carefully brushed Rosie's long coat.
"Rosie would like to say thank you," I told him.

I turned to Rosie and said, "Speak!" Rosie barked twice
to thank Peter for grooming her so well.

In the next room we met Alexander. Alexander was by himself because he was too sick that day to play with other children. Rosie loved Alexander right away.

The first thing she did was roll over on her back, so Alexander could rub her belly. That made Alexander laugh.

"Rosie looks like a shaggy rug!" he said.

Then Alexander lay down beside Rosie and they napped together awhile.

When they woke up, they shared some Cheerios. I told Alexander how to keep Rosie from grabbing them.

"Rosie, don't touch!" said Alexander.

Rosie turned her head away.

"Okay, take them!" Alexander said.

Rosie ate the Cheerios from Alexander's hand. Then she licked Alexander on the cheek and got a big hug in return.

A few weeks later a call came from The Village Nursing Home asking if Rosie would like to come and visit. We set up an appointment for the next afternoon.

Bea was the first person we met. Bea cannot use her arms or legs, and she has no feeling in them. Bea likes to watch Rosie and to feel Rosie's soft fur against her face.

Then we met Thomas. Thomas was in a wheelchair. Rosie made herself at home in his lap.

"She's cuddly, just like my grandson!" said Thomas.

Down the hall, we heard a woman crying.

"I have so many problems," she said.

"Maybe you'll feel better if you tell them to Rosie," I suggested. "Rosie is a very good listener."

"Rosie?" she asked. She wiped away her tears and started to smile. "My name is Rosie, too!"

The two Rosies had a good visit. Then Linda, a nurse, asked us to look in on Bill down the hall.

"Don't worry if he won't talk to you. He hasn't spoken to anyone in weeks. And he hardly eats. I think he's very lonely," she explained.

I brought Rosie to Bill's room.

"Would you like a visitor?" I asked.

Bill looked at Rosie, then turned away. But then he turned back. For a few minutes he just stared.

Finally he asked in a very quiet voice, "How can the little dog see?"

I told Bill how Rosie's long lashes hold up her hair to let her see through. Suddenly Bill was ready to visit. He had a lot to say about dogs with long hair, and the dog he had when he was a child, and how he wished he had his dog for company now.

I told Bill that Rosie would come visit him again soon. By the time we left, Bill did not seem so lonely anymore. He was saying to Linda, "My dog, Harley, loved to eat cherry Jell-O. Are we having Jell-O for dessert tonight?"

Linda was so happy, she said, "You will have Jell-O if I have to make it for you myself!"

When we left the nursing home, Rosie's tail was way up high and wagging. I offered her a drink of cool water. Then I lifted up her hair to look in her eyes. They were clear and bright.

"Rosie, you are a very good visiting dog," I said. "You are a very good friend."

Author's Note

Rosie, a Tibetan terrier, was trained at the ASPCA, received the American Kennel Club's Canine Good Citizenship Award, and is a Delta Society Pet Partner® and a member of Therapy Dogs International.

According to legend, Tibetan terriers were considered "holy dogs." They were raised in Tibetan monasteries by lamas or priests and were given as gifts, but never sold.

The first Tibetan terrier introduced to the Western world belonged to Dr. Agnes R. H. Greig, an English physician who in the 1930s was presented with a puppy for saving the life of a Tibetan woman.

A dog of any breed who has the right temperament and proper training may become a visiting dog. To find out about visiting dog programs in your area and the requirements for participating, call your local animal shelter or 4-H Club, or visit The Delta Society® at www.deltasociety.org.

Acknowledgments

Our thanks to the following people and organizations for generously offering their time and expertise:

Frank Bardin, The New York Hospital; Joan Marie Benedetto, The Village Nursing Home, NYC; James A. Corrao, D.V.M.; Rosa Corrello, Jennie Knauff Children's Center; Maureen Fredrickson, The Delta Society; Jeff Goldstein and the Kidwitness News Team, P.S. 41, Brooklyn, N.Y.; Randi Haberkorn, D.V.M.; Sally Haddock, D.V.M.; Vivian Harris, Ronald McDonald House; Sister Angelus Healy, The Lavelle School for the Blind; Betty Jackson, The Muscular Dystrophy Association; Mary Ann Koutzis, Jennie Knauff Children's Center; Erica Leeuwenburgh, Tomorrow's Children's Institute, Hackensack Medical Center; Eda Lepelstat, District 75/ Citywide Programs, NYC Board of Education; Patricia Lopez, The Lavelle School for the Blind; Debra Mason, The Lighthouse, Inc.; Mary McCready, The New York Hospital; Pamela Macdonald, Bellevue Hospital; Kirvy McMurry, The Village Nursing Home, NYC; Pat Mulholland, P.S. 138M, NYC; Ronald Napal, United Cerebral Palsy of NYC, Inc.; Nancy O'Connell, The Associated Blind, Inc.; Renee Perkins, Jennie Knauff Children's Center; Kathy Sanders, P.S. 138M, NYC; U.S. Color Lab, Inc., NYC; Elizabeth Teal, ASPCA.

There are others who have helped enormously: our patient and supportive family and friends; the warm and enthusiastic staff at Clarion Books; the exceptional people we met on our visits, who were anywhere from two to ninety-two years old; and the many kind people we met along the way, who stopped to pet and play with Rosie, letting her know the world is a friendly place to be. We thank you all.

Stephanie Calmenson
Justin Sutcliffe